CAMBRIDGE LIBRARY COLLECTION

Books of enduring scholarly value

Spiritualism and Esoteric Knowledge

Magic, superstition, the occult sciences and esoteric knowledge appear regularly in the history of ideas alongside more established academic disciplines such as philosophy, natural history and theology. Particularly fascinating are periods of rapid scientific advances such as the Renaissance or the nineteenth century which also see a burgeoning of interest in the paranormal among the educated elite. This series provides primary texts and secondary sources for social historians and cultural anthropologists working in these areas, and all who wish for a wider understanding of the diverse intellectual and spiritual movements that formed a backdrop to the academic and political achievements of their day. It ranges from works on Babylonian and Jewish magic in the ancient world, through studies of sixteenth-century topics such as Cornelius Agrippa and the rapid spread of Rosicrucianism, to nineteenth-century publications by Sir Walter Scott and Sir Arthur Conan Doyle. Subjects include astrology, mesmerism, spiritualism, theosophy, clairvoyance, and ghost-seeing, as described both by their adherents and by sceptics.

True History of the Ghost

Chemist and illusionist John Henry Pepper (1821–1900) lectured at the Royal Polytechnic Institution in London, and incorporated experiments, illusions and magic lanterns into his popular science lectures. In 1862 he developed a stage-show illusion called 'the ghost'. This involved using strategically placed pieces of glass and specific lighting in order to create the illusion of ghostly figures on stage. The illusion was immensely popular in the second half of the nineteenth century – it was visited by royalty, and Pepper's show toured to America, Canada and Australia. In this book, first published in 1890, Pepper details the history of 'the ghost' and the process of carrying out the illusion. 'Pepper's Ghost' is considered to be a precursor to cinema, and this book will be of interest to those studying the development of popular nineteenth-century culture, the 'entertainment industry', and the origins of cinema.

Cambridge University Press has long been a pioneer in the reissuing of out-of-print titles from its own backlist, producing digital reprints of books that are still sought after by scholars and students but could not be reprinted economically using traditional technology. The Cambridge Library Collection extends this activity to a wider range of books which are still of importance to researchers and professionals, either for the source material they contain, or as landmarks in the history of their academic discipline.

Drawing from the world-renowned collections in the Cambridge University Library, and guided by the advice of experts in each subject area, Cambridge University Press is using state-of-the-art scanning machines in its own Printing House to capture the content of each book selected for inclusion. The files are processed to give a consistently clear, crisp image, and the books finished to the high quality standard for which the Press is recognised around the world. The latest print-on-demand technology ensures that the books will remain available indefinitely, and that orders for single or multiple copies can quickly be supplied.

The Cambridge Library Collection brings back to life books of enduring scholarly value (including out-of-copyright works originally issued by other publishers) across a wide range of disciplines in the humanities and social sciences and in science and technology.

True History
of the Ghost

And All About Metempsychosis

JOHN HENRY PEPPER

CAMBRIDGE
UNIVERSITY PRESS

CAMBRIDGE UNIVERSITY PRESS

Cambridge, New York, Melbourne, Madrid, Cape Town,
Singapore, São Paolo, Delhi, Mexico City

Published in the United States of America by Cambridge University Press, New York

www.cambridge.org
Information on this title: www.cambridge.org/9781108044349

© in this compilation Cambridge University Press 2012

This edition first published 1890
This digitally printed version 2012

ISBN 978-1-108-04434-9 Paperback

THE TRUE HISTORY

OF

THE GHOST.

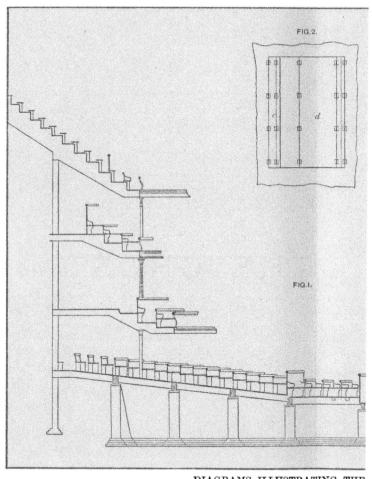

FIG.2.

FIG.1.

DIAGRAMS ILLUSTRATING THE
(From a drawing by Mr.

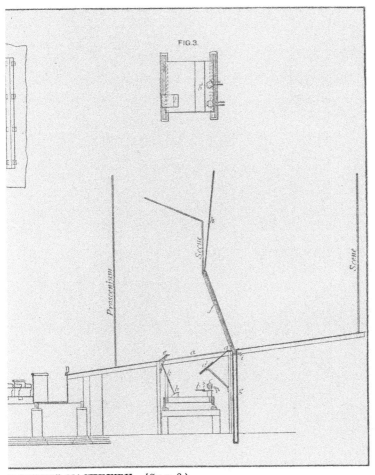

FIG. 3.

"GHOST" MACHINERY. (*See p.* 8.)
Barnard Chalon.)

THE TRUE HISTORY

OF

THE GHOST;

AND

ALL ABOUT METEMPSYCHOSIS.

BY

PROFESSOR PEPPER,

AUTHOR OF "CYCLOPÆDIC SCIENCE SIMPLIFIED," "THE PLAYBOOK
OF METALS," AND "BOY'S PLAYBOOK OF SCIENCE," ETC. ETC.

CASSELL & COMPANY, LIMITED:

LONDON, PARIS, NEW YORK & MELBOURNE.

1890.

POLYTECHNIC,

309, Regent Street, London, W.,

Christmas, 1889.

To WALTER HUGHES, Esq.,

Messrs. Hughes, Masterman, & Rew,

59, New Broad Street.

MY DEAR SIR,

Will you allow me to dedicate this little work to you, as some small recognition of the patience, care, and legal knowledge you displayed in bringing to a successful issue the difficult proceedings before the Attorney-General, Sir Roundell Palmer (now Lord Selborne), and also those in Chancery, connected with the sealing of my Ghost Patent by order of the late Lord Chancellor Westbury, in September, 1863?

With a grateful sense of the personal kindness and attention I have received from yourself and the other members of your Firm,

I am, my dear Sir,

Your old Client and sincere Friend,

THE AUTHOR.

TRUE HISTORY OF THE GHOST.

WHEN the Hyde Park second Great Exhibition in 1862 had closed its doors, and the reaction from the bustle attendant on the arrival and departure of country visitors had set in, so that the halls and lecture rooms lately crowded with the numerous patrons of the old Royal Polytechnic were somewhat deserted, there came to the aid of the Institute a new invention, which people by common consent called " The Ghost."

The latter was matured in this wise :—Mr. Dircks, a patent agent, who had saved some property and was an independent man, wrote a paper for the *Athenæum Literary Journal*, in which he described an optical effect that could be performed with sheets of glass. This paper excited no attention because the explanation of it was somewhat vague and unsatisfactory. The Christmas of 1862 was fast approaching, when Messrs. Horne, Thornthwaite, and Wood, philosophical instrument makers, of Newgate Street, invited the author to see a model which Mr. Dircks had caused to be constructed. This was the beginning of the Ghost; but as Mr. Dircks said that an entirely new theatre must be built to show the effects which he allowed could only be seen by a few people placed in an upper gallery, and then only by *daylight*, it was no wonder that the Crystal Palace, the Colosseum, and other places had all declined to have anything to do with Mr. Dircks or his model, which was now placed in the hands of Professor Pepper—so called because the Directors

B

of the then Royal Polytechnic had determined that his title should be Professor of Chemistry and Honorary Director of the above Institution. The title was not that of a hairdresser or a dancing-master, but was conferred upon him by express minute of the Board of Directors. Professor Pepper had had his services in establishing classes at the Royal Polytechnic already recognised by the authorities at South Kensington, who gave him an honorary diploma in Physics and Chemistry of the Committee of Council on Education some two or three years before the ghost was brought out, and at a time when he was sole lessee of the Polytechnic at a rental of £2,480 per annum, which had to be paid before a single lecture or entertainment was brought before the public. The classes Mr. Pepper established were for the study of Drawing, French, German, Arithmetic, and Mathematics, with, of course, Chemistry and Physics; and pupils were admitted at very low fees in order to encourage the working men to attend. He also arranged Monday evening lectures for the working classes, and reduced the admission to sixpence if the workmen came with proper tickets supplied by Professor Pepper, but signed by the foreman under whom the men worked.

All this took place about the years 1858—9, and was continued until the Institute finally closed its doors, principally caused by the fall of the stone staircase, and sold all off to a new limited liability company when Mr. Pepper was giving courses of lectures at the Crystal Palace, Sydenham. Again, for the last time, and during the absence of Professor Pepper in Australia, where he stopped ten years, viz., from 1879 to 1889, a sale of the plant and machinery, &c., of the Royal Polytechnic took place, on the 28th of February and three following days in 1882. Mr. George Buckland and his friends tried to secure the lease by purchase; but, not completing the purchase in time, it was

bought by Quintin Hogg, Esq., who has greatly added to
the size of the building, which is chiefly devoted to classes,
at least fifty in number, teaching all kinds of useful knowledge, with a large day school for boys, who are numbered
by hundreds, and are well and most efficiently taught by
competent masters. The Laboratory has also been en-
larged, and is now under the able guidance of Mr. Ward,
the teacher of Chemistry and Physics.

But to return to the Christmas of 1862, ever memorable
in the annals of the Institute because Mr. Pepper brought
out the illusion in quite a different manner from that con-
templated by Mr. Dircks, and so improved and simplified
the ghost that it could be shown in any lecture hall or theatre,
if sufficiently large to contain the necessary apparatus.

The following is a narrative from the lips of the inventor
of the ghost improvement:—"Just before Christmas Day
in 1862, I invited a number of literary and scientific friends,
and my always kind supporters, the members of the press,
to a private view of the new illusion to be introduced into
Bulwer's romantic and dramatic literary creation, called 'A
Strange Story.' The effect of the first appearance of the
apparition on my illustrious audience was startling in the
extreme, and far beyond anything I could have hoped for
and expected, so much so that, although I had previously
settled to explain the whole *modus operandi* on that evening,
I deferred doing so, and went the next day to Messrs. Carpmael, the patent agents, and took out a provisional patent
for the ghost illusion, in the names, at my request, of Dircks
and Pepper. The day after the first evening I showed the
ghost, Mr. Dircks came down to the Polytechnic, and after
saying how much pleased he was with the manner in which
I had introduced the illusion, ended by handing me a
letter, in which he spoke highly of my work in respect of
the ghost, and gave me spontaneously whatever profits
might accrue from the invention. Moreover, he went to

B 2

Carpmael with me, and, being an old and experienced patent agent himself, assisted in drawing up the patent which is here copied, with my original drawing of the improved method of showing the ghost by the use of a 'Double Stage,' at the old Royal Polytechnic Institute."

A.D. 1863, *5th February.* N° 326.

APPARATUS FOR EXHIBITING DRAMATIC AND OTHER PERFORMANCES.

LETTERS PATENT to Henry Dircks, of Blackheath, in the County of Kent, Civil Engineer, and John Henry Pepper, of No. 309, Regent Street, in the County of Middlesex, Professor of Chemistry, and Honorary Director of the Polytechnic Institution, for the Invention of "IMPROVEMENTS IN APPARATUS TO BE USED IN THE EXHIBITION OF DRAMATIC AND OTHER LIKE PERFORMANCES."

Sealed the 25th September 1863, in pursuance of an Order of the Lord Chancellor, and dated the 5th February 1863.

PROVISIONAL SPECIFICATION left by the said Henry Dircks

and John Henry Pepper at the Office of the Commissioners of Patents, with their Petition, on the 5th February 1863.

We, HENRY DIRCKS, of Blackheath, in the County of Kent, Civil Engineer, and JOHN HENRY PEPPER, of No. 309, Regent Street, in the County of Middlesex, Professor of Chemistry, and Honorary Director of the Polytechnic Institution, do hereby declare the nature of the Invention for "IMPROVEMENTS IN APPARATUS TO BE USED IN THE EXHIBITION OF DRAMATIC AND OTHER LIKE PERFORMANCES," to be as follows :—

The object of our said Invention is by a peculiar arrangement of apparatus to associate on the same stage a phantom or phantoms with a living actor or actors, so that the two may act in concert, but which is only an optical illusion as respects the one or more phantoms so introduced.

The arrangement of the theatre requires in addition to the ordinary stage a second stage at a lower level than the ordinary one, hidden from the audience as far as direct vision is concerned; this hidden stage is to be strongly illuminated by artificial light, and is capable of being rendered dark instantaneously whilst the ordinary stage and the theatre remain illuminated by ordinary lighting. A large glass screen is placed on the ordinary stage and in front of the hidden one.

The spectators will not observe the glass screen, but will see the actors on the ordinary stage through it as if it were not there; nevertheless the glass will serve to reflect to them an image of the actors on the hidden stage when these are illuminated, but this image will be made immediately to disappear by darkening the hidden stage. The glass screen is set in a frame so that it can readily be moved to the place required, and it is to be set at an inclination to enable the spectators, whether in the pit, boxes, or gallery, to see the reflected image.

The glass is adjustable and it is readily adjusted to the proper inclination, by having a person in the pit and another in the gallery to inform the party who is adjusting the glass when they see the image correctly.

SPECIFICATION filed in pursuance of the conditions of the Letters Patent, and of an Order of the Lord Chancellor, by the said Henry Dircks and John Henry Pepper in the Great Seal Patent Office on the 31st October 1863.

To ALL TO WHOM THESE PRESENTS SHALL COME, we, HENRY DIRCKS, of Blackheath, in the County of Kent, Civil Engineer, and JOHN HENRY PEPPER, of No. 309, Regent Street, in the County of Middlesex, Professor of Chemistry, and Honorary Director of the Polytechnic Institution, send greeting.

WHEREAS Her most Excellent Majesty Queen Victoria, by Her Letters Patent, bearing Date the Fifth Day of February, in the year of our Lord One thousand eight hundred and sixty-three, in the twenty-sixth year of Her reign, did, for Herself, Her heirs and successors, give and grant unto us, the said Henry Dircks and John Henry Pepper, Her special licence that we, the said Henry Dircks and John Henry Pepper, our executors, administrators, and assigns, or such others as we, the said Henry Dircks and John Henry Pepper, our executors, administrators, and assigns, should at any time agree with, and no others, from time to time and at all times thereafter during the term therein expressed, should and lawfully might make, use, exercise, and vend, within the United Kingdom of

Great Britain and Ireland, the Channel Islands, and Isle of Man, an Invention for "Improvements in Apparatus to be used in the Exhibition of Dramatic and other like Performances," upon the condition (amongst others) that we, the said Henry Dircks and John Henry Pepper, our executors or administrators, by an instrument in writing under our or their hands and seals, or under the hand and seal of one of us or them, should particularly describe and ascertain the nature of the said Invention, and in what manner the same was to be performed, and cause the same to be filed in the Great Seal Patent Office on or before the Third day of November, in the year of our Lord One thousand eight hundred and sixty-three.

Now Know Ye, that I, the said John Henry Pepper, on behalf of myself and the said Henry Dircks, do hereby declare the nature of the said Invention, and in what manner the same is to be performed, to be particularly described and ascertained in and by the following statement thereof, that is to say :—

The nature and object of our said Invention is by a peculiar arrangement of apparatus to associate on the same stage a phantom or phantoms with a living actor or actors, so that the two may act in concert, but which is only an optical illusion as respects the one or more phantoms so introduced.

The arrangement of the theatre requires in addition to the ordinary stage a second stage at a lower level than the ordinary one, hidden from the audience as far as direct vision is concerned; this hidden stage is to be strongly illuminated by artificial light, and is capable of being rendered dark instantaneously whilst the ordinary stage and the theatre remain illuminated by ordinary lighting. A large glass screen is placed on the ordinary stage and in front of the hidden one. The spectators will not observe the glass screen, but will see the actors on the ordinary stage through it as if it were not there; nevertheless the glass will serve to reflect to them an image of the actors on the hidden stage when these are illuminated, but this image will be made immediately to disappear by darkening the hidden stage. The glass screen is set in a frame so that it can readily be moved to the place required, and it is to be set at an inclination to enable the spectators, whether in the pit, boxes, or gallery, to see the reflected image. The glass is adjustable and it is readily adjusted to the proper inclination by having a person in the pit, and another in the gallery, to inform the party who is adjusting the glass when they see the image correctly.

Having thus stated the nature of our Invention, we will proceed more fully to describe the manner of performing the same.

DESCRIPTION OF THE DRAWINGS.—Fig. 1. (*Frontispiece*).

Figure 1 of the annexed Drawings illustrates the arrangement of a theatre for carrying our Invention into effect; the Figure shows a section taken through the stage, the orchestra, the pit, and gallery.

a, *a*, is an opening which is formed in the ordinary stage. In the front part of the stage, but at a lower level, is the hidden stage *b*. The opening *a* is capable of being closed at the top by trap doors, a plan of which is shewn at Figure 2. When the trap doors are closed, actors on the ordinary or visible stage can pass freely to and fro above the lower or hidden stage. The ordinary stage and trap doors are covered with green baize or other dark material, so that when the trap doors are opened, the audience, even those in the gallery, will not readily be able to perceive the opening. The actors or objects corresponding

with the phantom images, which it is desired to repre-
sent to the audience, are on the lower or hidden stage *b*,
and are strongly illuminated by the lime light or the electric
light, or other powerful illuminating means may be employed. This light must accompany the actor in any
movement he has to make. The hidden stage *b*, and the
lanterns *c*, may be mounted on a carriage on rails (a plan of
which is shown at Figure 3), so that when it is necessary
for the phantom actor or object on the lower stage
to be moved, the lanterns may be caused to move
also, or the lanterns may remain stationary whilst the actor
moves, provided the whole space through which he moves
is sufficiently illuminated. The lanterns are to be provided
with means for instantaneously extinguishing or masking
the light, and for reproducing it so that the phantom may
be made to disappear and reappear at pleasure, whilst the
audience and the ordinary stage will be more or less
lighted in the ordinary manner according to the effects
desired to be obtained. For this purpose a board b^1 is
employed, which is capable of being raised into the position
shewn by dotted lines so as entirely to cut off the light
from the hidden stage when desired, or an ordinary opaque
shade attached to each lantern may be used for the purpose, or when using the lime light the desired effects are
caused by gradually or instantaneously (as the case may
require) cutting off the supply of gases, and the phantom
image may by any of these means be caused gradually or
instantaneously to fade away. When the trap doors over
the hidden stage are open, the part *d* thereof assists in
hiding the lanterns and the opening from the audience.
The part *e* is raised into the position shown in the Drawing
and acts (together with the part *d*) to screen the lanterns
from the audience, and also to insure that any actor or
object on the hidden stage shall not accidentally appear
above the level of the visible stage. The phantom actor,

when standing on the stage *b*, leans against the screen *k*, which is inclined so as to be parallel with the glass screen, and is covered with black velvet or other dark material, as is also the stage *b*, in order that no image of either the screen *k* or the stage *b* may be seen in the reflection. *f* (the glass screen) is a large sheet of plate glass on the ordinary stage, of sufficient size to reflect the full length of the actors or objects on the hidden stage to the audience in the pit, boxes, and galleries of the theatre. The hidden stage is between the glass and the audience. The glass may be mounted in a swing frame so that it may be adjusted to the angle required, or it may readily be done by screws or ropes and pulleys, or otherwise. The glass screen is to be set at such an inclination as to bring the reflected image to the level of the visible or ordinary stage. This will enable the spectators, whether in pit, boxes, or gallery, to see the reflected image without any obstruction to the view above the foot lights, and it will be visible from all parts of the house except those extreme positions which cannot command a view through the glass of that part of the stage where the image is reflected.

The proper angle of inclination of the glass is ascertained experimentally by having persons in the different parts of the house to say when the image is shewn to them correctly. The scenery is so disposed as to conceal the frame of the glass, and we prefer that the glass should be able to descend into an opening or box *g* beneath the stage, in which case we counterbalance the glass and frame so that they may easily be raised into the position desired by means of a rope *h*, by which, aided by the bolts *i*, the glass is supported in the required position. The glass may either be adjusted when screened from the audience, and remain in position during the scene, or (the proper angle of inclination having been previously ascertained by experiment) the glass may be raised on to the ordinary or visible stage, and placed in position whilst the scene is before the eyes of the audience under a subdued light without the movement being observed, for which latter purpose the top bar of the frame of the glass should be made very light or be omitted altogether. This arrangement admits of an actor on the visible stage passing across the space which the glass is to occupy, and this he can do just before the appearance of the phantom, and then immediately the glass is run up, the trap doors are opened, the actor or image on the hidden stage is illuminated and the phantom appears. This arrangement will render it less likely that the audience should imagine that there is anything interposed between them and the actors than if the glass plate remained permanently in position during the scene. The hidden or lower stage may be provided with a well or hole up which an actor can rise; he will then appear as a spectre rising out of the visible stage. The lanterns may be provided with coloured glasses in order to heighten the effect. As the actors on the visible stage do not themselves see the spectral images, marks should be placed on the stage or other indications made in order that they may know the position which the spectres appearing to the audience are to occupy. In order to appear upright upon the visible stage the actor or object on the hidden stage should be inclined so as to be as nearly as practicable parallel with the surface of the glass screen. In effecting this assistance is afforded by the screen k of the hidden stage. Several sheets of glass may be similarly employed at the same time if one is not of sufficient width to cover the different parts of the stage at which it is desired that the spectre should appear, the interval or junction being concealed by the introduction of a tree or column or some other piece of scenery.

Having thus described the nature of our Invention and the manner of performing the same, we would have it understood that we make no claim to any of the parts separately, but what we claim is the combined arrangement as herein described of a glass inclined forwards towards the audience, and two stages, one the ordinary visible stage, and the other a hidden stage at a lower level than the ordinary visible stage and illuminated with a much stronger light than either the ordinary visible stage or the body of the house, and which light is capable of being instantaneously, or, if so required, gradually withdrawn and restored.

In witness whereof, I, the said John Henry Pepper, have hereunto set my hand and seal, this Thirty-first day of October, in the year of our Lord One thousand eight hundred and sixty-three.

J. H. PEPPER. (L.S.)

Returning to the author's narrative :—The Ghost illusion was first shown in what was called the small theatre of the Royal Polytechnic, but as the audience increased so rapidly it was removed by the following Easter and shown on a grander scale in the large theatre of the Institution, and where the dissolving views were usually exhibited.

The late Mr. O'Connor, of the Haymarket, painted the first scene used, representing the laboratory of " The Haunted Man," which Christmas story the late Charles Dickens, by his special written permission, allowed me to use for the illustration of the Ghost illusion. This ghost scene ran for fifteen months, and helped to realise, in a very short time, the sum of twelve thousand pounds, not counting what I received for granting licences to use the Ghost, and also the sums realised during many successive years as new ghost stories were brought out.

Sylvester now patented the use of looking-glass in the performance of the Ghost, which I thought very good, and bought of him—he could only infringe my patent by attempting to use it, and therefore his patent was useless to anybody else but myself.

Mr. King, of Bath, brought out what he termed a "New Patent Ghost"; but my solicitors, Messrs. Hughes, Masterman, and Hughes, very soon quashed the alleged patent by appearing against Mr. King, when he tried to get his patent passed before the Solicitor-General, the result of which is thus described by

THE

London New Music Hall Journal.

MANCHESTER, AUGUST 10, 1863.

WITHDRAWAL OF THE GHOST FROM THE LONDON NEW MUSIC HALL.

It is with unfeigned regret that I have to announce to my numerous patrons the withdrawal of the Ghost from the London New Music Hall. The reason is as follows :—My engagement with Mr. King, to whom a large sum of money was paid down, was with the understanding that he should personally superintend the first representation of the " Great Optical Illusion, the Marvellous Ghost," which, however, he failed to do, and to which is attributable the failure and disappointment which ensued. I also distinctly understood that his representation was free from any infringement of the right of patent, and that it was in every respect equal to the original production of Professor Pepper. I beg, therefore, in order to acquit myself from the odium of disappointment which may have been felt by the unusually large attraction which it has occasioned to " The London " during the past week, to state that I have received an intimation from Professor Pepper that Mr. King's representation is an infringement upon his own, and that I have no course left open to me but at once to bear the disappointment, and allow its immediate withdrawal. It is my intention, however, to seek redress in the proper quarter.

I therefore trust that my numerous friends will see the predicament in which I have been placed, and readily acquit me of all blame; assuring them that I am at all times, regardless of expense, anxious to secure the most sterling talent that can be procured, and to avoid anything in the shape of disappointment.

JAMES HARWOOD.

I now introduced a Miniature Ghost of a danseuse, which, being only about fifteen inches high, danced on the stage to the great amusement of my very numerous kind patrons.

I took out a provisional patent for this addition to the Ghost Mysteries, and shall reproduce it this Christmas at the Polytechnic.

A Manchester man, under the *nom de plume* of Kit Skewift, thus ridicules the efforts made by King to produce the Ghost at Manchester :—

"TH' GHOST!!!

" When aw wur a lad—(but that wurnt yesterday, nor th' day before, nor any day last wick)—aw used to be trayted neaw and then to wot wur cawd a good ghost story. Owd foak then wur vast fond o' ticklin' yung foaks' yers wi' tales abeawt hobgoblins, ghosts, carnivorous giants, vampyres, ogres, un aw macks o' uncouth beeins. Aw railly believe they thowt sitch tales wur profitable, morally un' religiously speighkin', un' had little thowt abeauwt th' uproar 'ut they caused amung eawr juvenoile nerves. Weel con aw remember beein' neaw un then freetunt till it wur th' herdest job i' th' world to keep my heart fro' other roisin' up into my meawth, or skutterin' deawn in t' clugs. My yure

would ha' stood up loike th' bristles uv a dleetin' brush, un'
th' best com ut ever wur made would ha' fawn a victim to
any attempt to smooth it deawn to its gradely place ; nay,
aw believe if anybuddy had tried wi' a par o' curlin' tungs to
make it twist, they'd ha' brokken um loike owd chips.
These tales gien me no partikilur noshun as to wot ghosts
wur ; praps th' tellers-had no very clear ideo theirsels ; but
aw geet o sort uv a general inklin' 'ut they wur a very quare,
a very extriordinary, un a very wilful set o' beeins ; some on
um vast fond uv a toidy practical joke ; un aw on um i'
their element when they wur potteriu' foaks' plucks to make
eawt wot the dickens they meant by their merlocks.

"For some days th' good foaks o'th' city o' Manchester
have had before their een uppo' th' waws, un' i'th' shop
windows, bills printed i' black un flarin' red ink, th' letters
big enoof welly for a bloint chap to see, anneawncin' at th'
Lunnun New Music Haw th' appearance uv a 'Mervellous
Ghost'—*King's* Ghost ! as a roival to that uv Professor
Pepper. Loike aw curious foak 'ut are made hongry wi'
expectashun, aw went th' other neet to have a look at it,
imaginin', as aw went alung through th' streets, that at last
aw should get a peep at a spectre uz would carry back my
moind to my yung days, un gie me some inseet into th'
naytur and essence uv sperrits—not sitch as one beighs at
th' keawnter uv a *vault*, but sitch as proceed fro' th' clay
tenement that lies, moshunless, decayin' within. Aw durnt
know but aw felt a little bit sayrious too, un' a tunchy bit
groiped wi' fear, for it met be that th' seet would be made
doubly awful by th' appearance uv my gronny's ghost ; if it
wur, un hoo seed me, hoo'd be shure t' gie me a blisterin
wi' hur tung, for hoo wur a raddler at takkin' th' sheighne
eawt on me wi' that glib little member uv hus. But when
th' ghost did appear—or *should* have appeart in its full
proposhuns, by th' mack aw fun' mysel as far fro th'
possesshun uv a genuine crumb o' ghostly wisdum uz ever

aw wur i' my born days. It should ha' bin an illustrious ghost—no less a chap than Owd Hamlet, th' suvverin uv anyshunt Denmark ; un' theerefore a rail *King's* ghost (beawt patent). But that may akeawnt fer its peevishness, its tricks, un' its uncommon way o' introducin' itsel'. It wouldn't appear aw at wonst ; at fust it showed its yed ; then, giving itsel' a wry neck, it lugged in its showders un its breast ; then it disappeart, un' shortly begun to ascend wi' its legs un' feet, or else a pair uz it had borrowed fro' a nayburin' corpse, uppermost ; un' when it had getten so far in seet as its sternum, it flittert abeawt in an ungrayshus manner, as if tryin' to doance th' Cure on its yed. Praps it wur *because* it wur a *King's* ghost that it wur so wilful, un' tried to be so unnatural in its ways, for some o' th' owd kings wur rum jockies, un', for owt we know, owd Hamlet met be loike owd George Thard, who, Byron says, geet into heaven by mistake, wi' his yed under his arm, not havin' any use for it in a place wheere good thowts un good principles are alone acceptable. Owd Hamlet met be labburin' under an idea that Lankishire wur a place in which a chap would be uv as mitch service to his felly crayturs when stonnin' on his yed as when reort up i' th' ushual style on his feet.

"This ghostly bizness is cawd an 'optical illushun.' Shouldn't it be cawd an 'optical *delushun*'? Aw know aw never seed as monny pairs o' optics so noicely chetted as there wur on this occashun. Professor Buck's kunjurashuns we know beforehond are nowt but decepshuns ; but aw'll be flogged if i'th' way o' bamboozlin' one's wits, un' makin th' sense uv seet counifogle aw eawr other senses, he isn't far ayed o' King's ghost—a very prince besoide a regilur muff.

"Neaw Pepper's ghosts, they say, are genuine, are wot they're professed to be—foine specimens uv wot true science un' profershunal skill con accomplish. When aw th' whole bevy o' King's ghosts are *mustert*, they're not,

placed alungsoide o' one *Pepper*, wuth so mitch as a pinch o'
sawt ; though, by th' way 'at they try to catch owd brids,
they met have a lerge stock on hond o' th' latter herticle.

"But, moind yoa, aw dunnot blame Mestur Harwood, th'
lesse o' th' Haw. Now, not I ; he, aw understond, has been
done as weel, nay to a bigger tune, than th' public ; un' that
he's doubly vext to think that he should, aimin' at producin'
every novelty 'ut's wuth presentin' to th' public, pay his good
money for a bad ghost! Un' to aw th' professhunals engaged at th' establishment it mun be awfully mortifyin' ; for
wot gives 'um th' horrors mooar than an ominous convicshun
that th' *ghost winnot wawk ?* Heawever, if awm reetly in-
formt, King's ghost is to vanish, un' Pepper's is to appear in
its place. This shows a determinashun not to be done wi'
a pousy Jack-o'-lantern.

"By th' *Music Haw Journal* aw see too that Stead, th'
original Cure, un' Mestur Ware, th' author uv so monny
comic sungs, are to appear next wick. Booath o' theese
chaps aw seed i' Lunnun, when aw went to look at th' Eggsi-
bishun ; un', my word, if they dunnot make Lankishire foak
lowf away aw unpleasant dreoms, un' shift aw th' bile left by
th' ghost, awm no judge, that's aw ! So, there's no need to
despair. As Shakspere says, ' Shadows avaunt ! ' un' make
way for substanshul entertainments.—Yours gradely,

"August 7, 1863.   KIT SKEWIFT."

Towards the end of May, 1863, the audiences increased
enormously at the Royal Polytechnic, so that it became
necessary to have a select afternoon performance, the admission fee being raised from 1s. to 2s. 6d. on Saturday mornings
only. It was at this period that I was honoured with a visit
from their Royal Highnesses the Prince and Princess of
Wales and suite ; and after the performance had been wit-
nessed by them, I showed the Prince and Princess how the
ghost was raised, and explained to my distinguished audience

c

all the machinery and appliances used. Some of the suite amused the Prince by becoming ghosts, and the following notice appeared the next morning in the *Times*, May 20th, 1863 :—

"Yesterday morning, by special command, Professor Pepper had the honour of delivering his ghost lecture before their Royal Highnesses the Prince and Princess of Wales, and the Prince and Princess Louis of Hesse, who were attended by the Countess of Macclesfield, Baroness Von Schenck, Major Teesdale, and Captain Westerweller. The distinguished party were received by Professor Pepper, and after being conducted round the galleries passed to the large theatre, where a commodious Royal box had been prepared for their reception. At the conclusion of the lecture, by the invitation of Professor Pepper, they went behind the scenes, and examined with much interest the machinery and appliances for producing the Polytechnic 'ghost.' At the conclusion, their Royal Highnesses graciously thanked the directors of the institution, and after shaking hands with Professor Pepper, retired."—*The Times, May 20th, London, England.*

"The ghosts of the Polytechnic, which manifest themselves as a startling appendix to Mr. Pepper's 'Strange Lecture' on optical illusions, have proved singularly attractive, and when the hour arrives for their appearance the lecture room becomes as crowded as the pit of a theatre on the night of Boxing-day."—(*Second Notice*), *The Times, Jan. 20th, London, England.*

The real element of success in the production of "The Strange Story," however, must be assigned to the ghost.

So many base and servile imitators now appeared with a sorry imitation of the Polytechnic ghost that it became necessary to send the following advertisement to all the London papers :—

" ADVERTISEMENT.

" Caution to persons pirating Professor Pepper's Ghost. —Messrs. Dircks and Pepper are the sole Patentees of the Ghost invention. The third and last hearing took place before Sir Roundell Palmer, the Solicitor-General, on Saturday the 15th August, 1863, when he decided in favour of Messrs. Dircks and Pepper."

I also addressed the following letter to the Press :—

" POLYTECHNIC INSTITUTION,
" 309, Regent Street, London,
" 21st *August*, 1863.

"To the Editor of ———
" Sir,
"On public grounds I venture to call your attention to the fact that many persons are now going about the country endeavouring to pirate effects to be produced by the apparatus patented by Mr. Dircks and myself, and to deceive the public by giving them an exhibition with which they are certain to be disgusted, and with which I have nothing to do. I beg to enclose one of the numerous statements I have received from different parts of the country alluding to the imposture now so commonly practised. I shall esteem it a favour if you would insert this and the accompanying statement in your valuable journal.
" I am, Sir,
"Your obedient Servant,
" JOHN HENRY PEPPER."

I won all the cases taken into Court against persons using my name in a fraudulent manner, and in one flagrant instance the Magistrates gave the impostor fourteen days' imprisonment for " getting money under false pretences."

The famous *savant* Mon. l'Abbé Moigné, of Paris, wrote

the brief notice of the ghost which is here copied from his journal called *Les Mondes*, May, 1863 :—

"NOUVELLES ET FAITS DIVERS.

"ROYAL POLYTECHNIC INSTITUTION.

"Les énergiques directeurs de l'Institution royale polytechnique ont inauguré une série de matinées fashionables amusantes du samedi qui, à en juger par les deux séances déjà données, promettent un très-heureux succès. On a surtout remarqué le leçon expérimentale de M. Pepper, sur le thallium, sur les merveilles de l'analyse spectrale, et la part qu'elle a eue à la découverte du nouveau métal. En raison du beau monde qu'elles devaient recevoir, les galeries avaient été tapissées et décorées avec goût de plantes exotiques rares. Comme intermède, on avait choisi le *Freischütz*, qui n'a rien perdu de sa fraîcheur et de son attrait, au triple point de vue musical, optique et humoristique. La semaine dernière, LL. AA. RR. le prince et la princesse de Galles ont fait une visite privée à cet incomparable établissement, et elles ont voulu qu'on les initiât aux mystères des fantômes. M. Pepper n'a pas cru pouvoir mieux répondre à leurs désirs qu'en faisant apparaître, sous forme de spectre, à leur grande surprise, une des personnes même de leur suite.

"Depuis que ce petit article a paru dans les journaux anglais, notre ami, M. Pepper, est venu installer à Paris, au théâtre impérial du Châtelet, le mystérieux appareil avec lequel il réalise ses apparitions fantastiques. De son côté, M. Robin a inauguré, samedi dernier, dans la salle déjà si fréquentée du faubourg du Temple, ses représentations de spectres vivants impalpables. L'attention publique étant ainsi vivement excitée, il nous semble que le moment est venu de rappeler l'article suivant inséré par nous dans le *Cosmos* de

1858, tome XIII, p. 563, et qui ne fut pas assez remarqué, parce que le moment n'était sans doute pas venu :—

" ' *Fantômes optiques.*—MM. Dircks et Pepper ont inventé une charmante disposition optique à l'aide de laquelle il fait apparaître des spectres et produit des illusions singulières. Il partage en deux compartiments, par une large glace sans tain, comme on en fait beaucoup aujourd'hui, la salle dans laquelle la scène doit se jouer. Dans le premier compartiment, en avant, il place les acteurs dont on ne devra voir que les images, destinées à représenter les spectres ou revenants ; dans le second compartiment, à droite, il installe les acteurs qui devront être vus en personne ; les spectateurs sont installés dans l'obscurité, au-dessus du premier compartiment en avant. Dans cette disposition, évidemment, si la scène commence, les spectateurs verront directement, à travers la glace, les acteurs du second compartiment ; its verront par réflexion seulement, ou dans leurs images formées au sein du premier compartiment et mêlés aux acteurs vus en personne, les acteurs situés au-dessous d'eux, dans le premier compartiment. Ces images refléchies, beaucoup moins lumineuses, feront l'effet d'ombres vivantes, d'êtres revenus de l'autre monde ; on pourra les faire avancer, rétrograder, sortir ou rentrer à travers les murs, en faisant varier la distance à la glace des acteurs qu'elles représentent, et l'on obtiendra des effets vraiment extraordinaires. C'est assurément une excellente idée.'

" C'est bien aussi là le secret de ces photographes spirites dont l'Amérique a eu l'initiative et qui ont tant fait de bruit."

And now Mr. Dircks, who had hitherto been most friendly to me, began to be otherwise, and to write me offensive letters, which I forbear to publish. Every morning and evening at the Royal Polytechnic I mentioned his name as a co-inventor. The daily programme always contained his name, and I can appeal to numbers who know me well that I have never attempted to borrow other people's honours from them, and if a discovery was made always gave to the person making it full credit for the same. It is certain that Dircks' apparatus was comparatively useless and that he knew nothing of the use of my double stage, and in fact the Solicitor-General, Sir Roundell Palmer, declined to grant a patent on Dircks' crude idea, as it was only when he understood the great improvement made by the use of the double stage and the employment of the electric light that he granted (as stated in the copy of the advertisement) at the third hearing the Ghost Patent which the Lord Chancellor subsequently ordered to be sealed after great opposition made by several Music Hall proprietors. It is a very curious fact that the original model which Horne, Thornthwaite and Wood sent me was stolen by some person, who in my absence gave a fictitious verbal order as if from the firm named, and I never saw it again. The thief could not, however, have derived much benefit from the robbery, as the model was more likely to lead the possessor in the wrong than the right direction. I suppose the model went to America or Australia, as my imitators in those countries mostly made a terrible fiasco of the ghost when they first attempted to show it.

The following notice by a newspaper, of which unfortunately the name was cut off and lost, gives a very fair criticism on the ghost and its inventors :—

"THE PATENT GHOST.

"MODERN researches in Spiritualism have led to one practical result—the discovery of a ghost. Not of an ordinary old-fashioned ghost, appearing in the midnight hour to people with a weak digestion, haunting graveyards and old country mansions, and inspiring romance-writers into the mischief of three-volume novels ; but of a well-behaved, steady, regular, and respectable ghost, going through a prescribed round of duties, punctual to the minute—a Patent Ghost, in fact. This admirable ghost is the offspring of two fathers, of a learned member of the Society of Civil Engineers, Henry Dircks, Esq., and of Professor Pepper, of the Polytechnic. To Mr. Dircks belongs the honour of having invented him, or, as the disciples of Hegel would express it, evolved him from out of the depths of his own consciousness ; and Professor Pepper has the merit of having improved him considerably, fitting him for the intercourse of mundane society, and even educating him for the stage. After having bowed to the public at the Polytechnic Institution, he some weeks ago made his *début* upon the boards of the Britannia Theatre, in a new and highly original drama, entitled, ' The Widow and Orphans,—Faith, Hope, and Charity,' in which piece he continues to present himself nightly to crowded audiences with the greatest imaginable success.

" Possibly, all Britons do not know where the Britannia Theatre is situated, and it may not be necessary, therefore, to state that it has its place in the metropolitan suburb of Hoxton, inhabited chiefly by toy-makers and doll-dressers, and marked under the letter N by the Postmaster-General. Sceptics may smile at the idea of a Patent Ghost making his first appearance in a neighbourhood so little fashionable, and so far removed from the residence of Master Home, commander-in-chief of spirits and mediums, and solicitor-general of demons, ghosts, and shadows of the universe. It is no mere accident ; for it appears that there are good spiritual reasons why the ghost should have come out at Hoxton and nowhere else. Here, in this toy-making quarter, there lived, about a hundred years ago, a worthy citizen and officer of the Lord Mayor, Mr. Francis Bancroft, who was haunted all his life long with the one great idea that his body was predestined to arise visibly from the dead, and to wander over British earth in the shape of a tangible ghost. So deeply impressed was he with this belief that, while walking

in the flesh, his chief object was to take measures towards in-
suring his safe and speedy resurrection. With considerable
faith in the celebrated maxim of Luther's active Roman an-
tagonist, indulgence-selling Monk Tetzel :

> *' Sobald das Geld im Kasten klingt*
> *Die Seel' aus dem Fegfeuer springt '*—*

citizen Bancroft took great care, during his mortal career, to
accumulate a respectable amount of cash with the object of
forming a bribe for the guardians of his body. Accordingly,
in his will he left the sum of twenty-eight thousand pounds
for the establishment of schools and almshouses, with this
proviso, that his body should be ' preserved within a shew-
glass ' in the church."

During the time I was in Paris, and arranging the ghost for
exhibition at the Théâtre du Châtelet under Mons. Hostein,
I was surprised to find that the conjuror, Mons. Robin, was
showing the ghost at his séances. My lawyers interviewed
him, and discovered that, some years before, a little toy had
been brought out and patented in France by which a miniature ghost could be shown. It consisted of a box with a
small sheet of glass, placed at an angle of forty-five degrees,
and it reflected a concealed table, with plastic figures, the
spectre of which appeared behind the glass, and which
young people who possessed the toy invited their com-
panions to take out of the box, when it melted away, as it
were, in their hands and disappeared.

In France at that time all improvements on a patent fell
to the original patentee, and under that law I lost the
patent in France ; but Mons. Hostein honourably paid me
a large sum of money for the use of my improved ghost at
the Théâtre du Châtelet, Paris. Query.—Had Mr. Dircks'

---

* As soon as the money rattles in the boxes,
The soul jumps out of purgatory.

patent agent, in his searches after patents, ever come across the toy invented in Paris? Because it is substantially the ghost apparatus and produced that illusion; and thus it shows how correct are the words of Solomon, who has told us " There is nothing new under the sun."

If the reader will consult a book written by me, entitled " Cyclopædic Science Simplified," formerly published by Messrs. Frederick Warne and Co., but now bought and published by Messrs. Lippincott, the great American publishers of Philadelphia, Pa., U.S.A., he will find a very near approach to the ghost apparatus copied from Robinson's " Recreative Memories " published in 1831. The same author describes how the famous magician (so-called) Nostrodamus deceived even the astute and wily Marie de' Medicis by a vision which appeared in a looking-glass. Moreover, Sir Walter Scott, in his beautiful poem, " The Lay of the Last Minstrel," has introduced the use of mirrors for producing ghostly appearances, in the vision seen by the ill-fated Earl of Surrey, in the mirror huge and high of Cornelius ; the vision being " That fair and lovely form, the Lady Geraldine " (verses 16, 17, 18, 19, 20, canto vi.).

Before travelling about so much I had a trunk full of letters referring to the ghost illusion, many treating it as a supernatural phenomenon, and not an effect from natural causes.

In about four months my secretary wrote at least 1,000 letters in answer to those addressed to me.

I was offered house property in exchange for the right to exhibit the ghost and a full description of the apparatus on attendance at the Polytechnic to see how things were manipulated.

I publish one of the most amusing letters, which has no address or proper signature, but only the initials "R. C." :—

"Whereas the directors and managers of the Polytechnic

Institution believe and maintain the phenomenon called 'spirit-rapping' to be produced by trickery, jugglery, or some natural agency, and to be an imposture, I, the undersigned, on the contrary maintain that there is some non-human agent which moves the tables, chairs, etc., and carries on an intelligent conversation with spectators by knocking, or tilting, or other signs. I am ready to wager from £5 to £50 with any one who chooses to accept my challenge that the phenomenon shall take place, and that no one present shall be able to detect any sort of trickery or jugglery in the matter. It is to be clearly understood that mere opinions that the thing is done by natural agency are to go for nothing. The natural agency *must be proved:* On the other hand I defy any one to produce the same phenomenon by natural agency *without my being able to detect that agency.* In making this proposal I wish it to be distinctly understood that I do not place any trust or confidence in the so-called 'spirits,' as I maintain, in opposition to the whole body of so-called 'spiritualists,' that the intelligent agent which moves the tables, chairs, etc., and converses and answers questions by knocking, is nothing more or less than *the evil spirit* which dwells in humanity, and is found in every human being. This proposition can be clearly demonstrated. As to the so-called 'spirits' being the 'souls of the dead,' the idea is absurd, and this absurdity also can be made abundantly manifest. This spiritualism is doing an immensity of mischief, and ought to be exposed, but it will never be exposed if people shut their eyes *to the fact.* It will not be the less a fact, and will not the less impose on all who witness it, because there are men and women who *predetermine* in their own minds that it cannot be true, and refuse to be convinced *by either their senses or their understandings.* In all ages there have been deaf adders whom no music could charm, and there are in these days also many 'who having eyes will not see, and who having ears will not

hear.' *On what grounds* does any one assume as a cer-
tainty that such a thing is impossible?

"RICHARD CRUIN."

"If any one is so unwise as to be willing to pay £100 in
the event of the phenomenon taking place in his presence,
and of his being unable to detect any imposture, I undertake
that the · 'medium' shall exhibit *in any private room, in
any home, and with any furniture* (provided it be not too
heavy), and that the said medium shall submit *to be searched
both before and after the exhibition.*

"Nothing is easier than to lift a table by means of a concealed apparatus. The knocking also may be produced by
means of muscular motion or otherwise. But can any one
lift a table *without any apparatus,* simply by placing the
hand on it; or can any one contrive an apparatus so
cunning that no one present, having full liberty to examine
everything, shall be able to detect it?

"By collusion or otherwise questions also might be
answered, but I maintain that the agent in spiritualism can
tell all the most secret and hidden things of one's life, and
even one's secret thoughts, and also that it understands
and can converse *in any language.* I have verified this *by
repeated experience.* But it will not always speak when it is
wanted to speak, and the 'medium' has no power over it
to make it answer questions. But the fact that it often tells
lies and often refuses to tell anything, does not make void
the fact that it does also at times answer *every question
which one can ask it.* It is by this sort of capricious
behaviour that it succeeds in completely deluding some to
trust in it, and others to disbelieve in it altogether. But
let a man confine himself at first to the physical phenomenon
and try if he can make a table to rise up into the air completely off the ground, simply by placing his hand on it,
and *without any apparatus whatever.* If he cannot do this,

and if no human being can do it, let it be acknowledged
that there is some non-human agent. A little experience
will very soon convince any one that it is an intelligent,
and a wonderfully intelligent, agent, and then it will remain
to be considered whether this intelligent agent is good or
evil—*I say it is evil.*   R. C."

During the year 1863, when the ghost illusion was one
of the topics of the day, the famous George Cruikshank
wrote a pamphlet, entitled—" A Discovery concerning
Ghosts, with a Rap at the 'Spirit Rappers,' illustrated with
Cuts, and dedicated to the 'Ghost Club.'" Curious to say,
he says nothing respecting the Polytechnic ghost, but is
exercised chiefly with famous stories of ghosts and appari-
ions, which it is alleged have appeared to various persons.
The author examines analytically a number of them, and
comes to the conclusion that the persons relating them
usually deceived themselves or other people, and that most
of the stories are mental hallucinations. The inimitable
George, as his friends delighted to call him, treats with pro-
found contempt the spirit rappers, and all the cheats and
fortune-telling mendicants who try to impose on innocent
people with their bad conjuring tricks—people who might
have got through the world safely; but the fatal chord is
struck, and they go from bad to worse, until they end in
a mad house.

The whole tribe of persons who made money directly
or indirectly out of what they called spirit mediums, &c.,
fairly howled upon me in the lecture room, and, threatening
personal violence, I was for some time attended home at
night by the most stalwart of our Polytechnic employés ; for,
like Cruikshank, I vigorously denounced the traders in
spirits, founding my arguments on the belief that God was
too merciful to us to add to the troubles of this world the
fear and trembling brought about by pretended communica-
tion with the invisible world.

The first story I told at my Polytechnic "Strange Lecture" had a very simple plot.

It represented the room of a student who was engaged burning the midnight oil, and, looking up from his work, sees an apparition of a skeleton. Resenting the intrusion he rises, seizes a sword or a hatchet which is ready to his hand, and aims a blow at the ghost ; which instantly disappeared again and again to return.

This ghost was admirably performed by my assistant, whom we called Ye Perringe, who, wearing a cover of black velvet, held the real skeleton in his arms and made the fleshless bones assume the most elegant attitudes, the lower part from the pelvis downward being attired in white linen, and the white skeleton ghost assuming a sitting posture, so that it appeared to come out of the floor.

Although this exhibition only lasted a few minutes, it drew hundreds and thousands of pounds to the treasury of the Polytechnic. In fact, as already stated, I was obliged to remove to the larger theatre of the Institute.

The next ghost story was told in the large theatre ; and it illustrated Charles Dickens's story of the " Haunted Man." At the same time was shown " Cupid and the Love-Letter." When the curtain drew up, a peasant girl was discovered using her spinning-wheel and demurely thinking of something not told to the audience.

The ghost of a very pretty little boy dressed as Cupid now appears at her elbow, and discharges an arrow from his bow, which pierces the heart of the susceptible village girl. She attempts to caress the pretty Cupid, who eludes her kind advances, and is now discovered on the other side. The maiden turns to kiss him, but he is gone. At last, relenting, Cupid gives her a love-letter from some affectionate swain, which she takes and shows triumphantly to the audience, and leaving the girl to read it, the curtain again descended. These two illustrations of the ghost illusion ran for fifteen

months without alteration, and were succeeded by many others
—viz., Scrooge and Marley's Ghost, by Charles Dickens; the
Ghost of the diving bell; the knight watching his armour; the
poor author tested; the Ghost of Napoleon I. at St. Helena ;
and the Ghost in *Hamlet*, pronounced by a leading R.A. as
being nearly perfect, only wanting a little different colour in
the walls of the ramparts, which I adopted with his ultimate
satisfaction and approval.

The late Walter Montgomery took a great interest
in the ghost proceedings, and assisted me greatly in arranging the scenes with due regard to the dramatic art. There
is a mystery about his tragic end which deserves solution,
and his brother-in-law told me at Brisbane, Queensland,
that he did *not* commit suicide, but was shot by somebody
else.

The sands of the year 1863 had been nearly run
out, and I had taken the ghost to Manchester to a lecture
hall then under the skilful management of Mr. Peacock,
when another great success was scored—various London
theatres took out licences to use the ghost ; notably the
Haymarket, under Mr. Benjamin Webster ; The Britannia,
under Mr. and Mrs. Lane ; Drury Lane, under Mr. Chatter-
ton, also subsequently and after the famous ghost trial
before the Lord Chancellor. The Music Halls no longer
tried to infringe the patent, but those who required it
paid their fees for licences to do so.

The famous ghost trial came on in September at the
private residence of the Lord Chancellor Westbury, who
very graciously agreed to hear this patent case at once,
because his lordship was informed by my solicitor, Mr.
Walter Hughes, junr., that if he could not do so the
Polytechnic Ghost would most likely be swamped by the
multiplicity of imitators, good, bad, or indifferent.

Accordingly, one cold and chilly day I went down into
Hampshire, accompanied only by my solicitor, Mr. Walter

Hughes, junior, of the firm of Hughes, Masterman, and Hughes, 56, New Broad Street. On arrival we were shown into his Lordship's drawing-room, where, to my dismay, I found a little army of solicitors and barristers drawn up as if in battle array, and sitting in a row against the right-hand wall of the room.

His Lordship's secretary courteously came forward, and, noticing we were somewhat cold, placed chairs for us near the fire, and pulled up a table for our use on which to take notes.

We all rose respectfully when the Lord Chancellor entered, and, being requested by him to remain seated, the case was opened by his Lordship asking who appeared for the Plaintiffs, the music-hall proprietors. At least four answered, "I do, my Lord," and we in the minority could only give an answer from one voice—viz., that of my then young solicitor.

The music-hall people came down with two newspaper reporters to record their certain victory over me, but which, as it turned out, was a mistake, because the reporters could only tell the truth and record the verdict given in my favour.

The Lord Chancellor, so far as I can remember (and I have no notes), then addressed the Plaintiffs—

1st. I shall require you to show cause by what right or authority you appear before me this day.

2nd. I will hear you on the general merits of the case.

3rd. And lastly, on the novelty which the Defendant seeks to have completed under the protection of a Patent, and which novelty you appear to deny.

One of the barristers then rose, and after saying that he would bow with submission to anything his Lordship might suggest or rule, commenced his argument by calling attention to the fact that the number of days allowed by the Patent Law had already elapsed, and by sections so-and-so

I had lost the opportunity of getting the Patent sealed within the proper time allowed between granting Provisional Protection and sealing the Patent.

After he had ended, the Lord Chancellor asked if the Plaintiffs through their counsel had anything more to urge on this first point. They all bowed, and said " No."

His Lordship now said : " It is very true what you state respecting the wording of the Patent Act, *but* if you will turn to sections so-and-so you will find that the Law Officers of the Crown have full power to grant an extension of the time for completing and sealing the Patent on the proper application of the Defendant's solicitors, and as that application has already been made and granted, it must be evident that, though the Defendant exceeded the time usually allowed, he had full permission to do so from the constituted authorities. I will now hear you on the general merits of the case."

Here the learned counsel exhausted his law and rhetoric in making out there was really nothing to patent, for who could catch hold of a ghost? And more legal technicalities were advanced and argued than I can remember at this distance of time—viz., twenty-six years ago. However, his Lordship again asked, " Have you anything more to urge on this point?" and received the same reply, " No, my Lord, we have not." The Chancellor then replied *in extenso*, exposed all the sophistries of the arguments, and whilst complimenting the counsel on his learning and the care which he had bestowed upon the case, said again that there was nothing in the arguments that militated against the sealing of the Patent. Of course, they could take action at common law, and try the case before the judges appointed to try such cases if they thought proper, and, supported by affidavits resulting from a trial at common law, could bring the case again before him.

There was one point which the Lord Chancellor alluded to. He said: "Great stress had been laid on the impossibility of patenting a mere intangible nothing, viz., a ghost; but as he understood, the Defendant did not patent the shadowy result called the Ghost, but an apparatus for ' Exhibiting Dramatic and other Performances,' and without this apparatus no ghost could be rendered visible to an audience." His lordship then continued: " I will now hear you on the novelty of the proposed invention, which your affidavits declare is not new, but an imitation of something already exhibited."

The learned counsel now made various statements, supported apparently by affidavits from persons who alleged that they had seen the ghost a long time before, and, in fact, had used the very same apparatus I had employed or words to that effect. For instance, an old playbill emanating from the Old Tivoli Gardens, Margate—not perhaps the most refined place of entertainment, in fact, no ladies appeared to visit the place say, in 1851, when I heard a lady in tights discourse a song the burthen of which was—

" Take care, John Bull, or else you'll be done
In the Great Exhibition of '51."

The playbill was laid upon his Lordship's table, who, taking hold of it, asked, " Is this the playbill alluded to ? " and threw it on the floor. I suppose the counsel was not attending to some point of etiquette, and ought to have produced his playbill in the form of a High Chancery Court affidavit. The playbill alluded to a ghost that was to be shown, and counsel again called attention to their plan of the ghost apparatus, which he was instructed to say was the same or very similar to that used by Defendant. The affidavit of some other dramatic professional was also brought forward with several others ; but all things come to

D

an end, and at last the same distinct question rang out : " Have you anything more to urge on this question of novelty ? " with the answer as before. " No, your Lordship."

Lord Westbury commenced by alluding to the drawing brought forward by the Plaintiffs, and said, " I have examined the affidavit and the drawings, and find it is as nearly as possible a copy of the Defendant's own drawing deposited in confidence in the archives of the Patent Office, and when I visit that establishment will take care to enquire who has presumed to allow the Plaintiffs permission to copy the Defendant's original drawing of the apparatus used to show the ghost. I well remember," continued his Lordship, " being taken to the house of Belzoni, the distinguished traveller, and seeing an effect no doubt somewhat similar to that produced by the Defendant's apparatus, but I could not for one moment compare the toy of Belzoni with the refined and complete contrivances used by the Defendant at the Royal Polytechnic. An affidavit has been put in by the Plaintiffs, sworn to by a person calling himself a 'nigger minstrel.' He is elsewhere denominated an 'Ethiopian Serenader,' who had seen the Defendant's ghost shown years ago—a very respectable man, no doubt, in his vocation ; but to put the evidence of such a person against the affidavits of Michael Faraday, Sir David Brewster, and Professor Wheatstone, is a manifest absurdity. I, therefore, rule that the Great Seal of England be at once attached to the Defendant's patent, and that the Plaintiffs do pay the costs."

After certifying for the costs and having a little conversation with my solicitor and self, his Lordship withdrew, and we all went back to town. The reader can imagine my feelings of joy at the successful upshot of this trial when he learns that I had already received large sums for licences which I must have refunded if the case had gone against me.

For many years the ghost at the Polytechnic pursued its successful career, and earned £12,000 in a comparatively short space of time. I received an illuminated address of thanks, with a handsome honorarium, from the directors, and subsequently they presented my bust in marble to my late dear wife, with a letter from the Rev. J. B. Owen, M.A., the highly-gifted chairman of the old Royal Polytechnic.

Very few persons could understand how the ghost was produced, although many persons wrote about and explained it ; even the distinguished philosopher, Michael Faraday, when I took him behind the scenes, said, with his usual love of truth : "Do you know, Mr. Pepper, I really don't understand it." I then took his hand, and put it on one of the huge glass plates, when he said, "Ah ! now I comprehend it ; but your glasses are kept so well protected I could not see them even behind your scenes."

METEMPSYCHOSIS.

Since the ghost was produced at the Polytechnic years ago, the author has visited America, and seen not only the chief cities of the United States of America, but also those of patriotic Canada ; and about ten years ago, paying a casual visit to Messrs. Walker, the eminent organ builders, he enquired of Mr. James Walker what he had done with a model shown him during the height of the popularity of the ghost, by which an empty glass goblet, or one full of water, was gradually filled with, or changed into, wine (or coloured water resembling it), thus unwittingly and apparently embodying or putting into an illustrated form the miracle of the conversion of water into wine.

I was too busy and too well paid at the time to think of a new illusion, but I praised it much, and said if not

D 2

confined to too small stage limits, it was certainly as good, if not better, than the ghost illusion.

The time had now arrived when the London world was ready for something new (as commercial men would say) in the ghost line, and although Mr. James Walker, with the modesty of a truly scientific man, disclaimed the merit due to his invention, he did at last, at my request, throw himself, with the author, heart and soul into the production of the new illusion, which we called Metempsychosis. We now took out a patent for the new optical wonder, and having thus secured the invention from that piracy and robbery which too often dog the otherwise successful steps of inventors, causing nearly every patent to be called by the legal fraternity a *damnosa hereditas*, we looked about for a good place—hall or theatre—where the illusion could be started. None better could be thought of than the old Royal Polytechnic, where we offered at a moderate sum per week to produce it, paying for every stick, decoration, or engraved looking-glass ourselves. But it appeared that the funds of the institution were so reduced—it was supposed, by the immense expenditure on armies, warlike material, and ladies' legs required to produce a work emulating friend Barnum's gigantic "Nero," and called, with an alarming stretch of imagination, the "Siege of Troy," or "Destruction of Troy"—that the directors were unable to guarantee the weekly salary Mr. James Walker and myself demanded. Luckily for us, a percentage on the gross receipts was suggested, and brought in a great deal more money to our exchequer than the modest weekly salary would have given us. The public came in goodly numbers to see the new optical wonder, and all went well as long as the author remained in London and could devote his time and energies to the daily exhibition; but the time was now drawing rapidly near when, according to contract, he must leave for Australia.

Professor Pepper has invariably told his numerous patrons that, although obliged to keep secret for a reasonable time all optical illusions that he produced, he would ultimately tell the public all about it.

The metempsychosic era at the Polytechnic in 1879 was marked by the production of various stories, which were nicely edited and corrected by a lady of well-balanced, tasteful, and poetic mind—viz., by Miss Walker, the sister of the author's very able coadjutor.

The entertainment opened with a vacant stage, disclosing a sort of inner apartment about twelve feet square, tastefully upholstered, and closed by a curtain which could be lowered at pleasure, without interfering with the great roller and white curtain upon which Dissolving Views were shown. The author's adopted son, for he never had any children of his own, was now seen walking through the inner apartment to the foot-lights, where he bowed and, addressing the audience, had hardly got as far as the words, " Ladies and Gentlemen,—I am sorry to inform you that something has detained Professor Pepper——" when my voice was heard crying out : " Stop, stop ; I am here ! " and, appearing out of nothing and without the aid of trap doors or descent by the help of the copper wires, the author stood in the midst, and bowed his acknowledgments for the hearty greeting kindly given him by his audience. The entertainment now proceeded, and, after apologising for the gloom he was about to cast upon the meeting by the harassing story he was about to relate, finally stated that his subject would be those " fearful bags of mystery " called " sausages," remarking incidentally that though, thanks to Government analysts, many persons had heard of the examination and analyses of this dietetic refresher of the inner man, no one probably had ever seen sausages put together again, as it were, and formed into the very animal from which they were originally educed. A large white dish of sausages was now produced. They were placed in a wire basket, such as pot-plants are suspended in from windows and verandahs, and hung up in the inner chamber. About one minute elapsed; the sausages were gone, and out of the basket came the author's dear little sagacious white poodle, with his blue ribbon and little bells, wagging his tail, barking at the audience, and coming down to lick the hand of his master. The poor little creature was accidentally poisoned by eating bits of meat the rats had dropped whilst scuttling to their holes to die of the too rapid poison prepared by the author for those pests of domesticated people.

Then the metamorphoses proceeded. Oranges were changed into pots of marmalade, and given away to the boys, and a chest of tea was converted into a tray carrying a steaming teapot, sugar, milk, cups of tea, and handed by the attendants to the ladies in the *reserved* seats only—such is the blighting influence of cash, which caused the one-shilling people to be neglected and the eighteenpenny-reserved-seat folks to have their teas. The ghost of Banquo in "Macbeth," and the ditto in "Hamlet" followed, with the curious change of a deserted piano into one at which played and sang a living member of the fair sex, attended by a gentleman in faultless black coat and white tie, who turned over her music; and this Part I. wound up with the change of a gentleman into a lady, who walked down to the footlights, sang a song, and then vanished into "thin air."

But all these changes could only happen in the smaller inner apartment, the actors might walk anywhere else at pleasure, and out of the charmed circle Walker could not change to Pepper, or the latter refer to the living beings when they faded out of sight as regular "Walkers."

So much for what was done, and now the anxious reader is getting impatient, and if a lady is doubtless curious (the poor men never are so) to know how it was all done, and as the illusion has apparently left the domain of optical science and is now relegated to the conjuring profession, the author has no hesitation in fulfilling his long-ago promise made to the public to let, as Mr. Cremer, jun., says in his most amusing book on " Conjuring," the cat out of the bag.

Before the illusion can please the eyes, the proper apparatus for producing it must be constructed ; and the key to the result consists in the use, not of clear plate glass employed in the ghost illusion, but of engraved silvered glass.

Ordinary looking-glass, such as is used for common mirrors or looking-glasses, is usually made by attaching an amalgam of tin-foil and quicksilver to one side of a clean sheet of plate or other glass.

Glass prepared in this way cannot be successfully engraved, and when the chisel or other tool is drawn with pressure across it, is liable to chip ; and instead of clear, sharp engraved lines being obtained, they are ragged, and, in most cases, large patches of the amalgam are torn off.

This is not the case when glass really silvered by successful chemical processes is used, and when pure metallic silver is precipitated on to the surface of the best and flattest plate glass. When Mr. Walker and myself commenced our experiments in March, 1879, the so-called " Patent Silvered Glass" was expensive and confined to moderate-sized pieces of plate glass. Our first care, therefore, was to construct a table that could be brought by screws to a perfect level, and one that would carry a plate of glass at least twelve feet six long by six feet eight wide. Such a plate being most carefully cleaned, and quite free from grease, was placed upon the table, and levelled by means of spirit levels, just as a plate of glass used for the old collodion process would be levelled, in order that the fluid should not run off at one edge, leaving the other comparatively dry; and now came the knotty point—Which was the best silvering process to use? On consulting the best records of this art, we found valuable information in the *English Mechanic*, Vol. xxi., No. 542.

The reader will find the following process very successful if minutely carried out in all its technical details—

To Silver Glass.

Prepare two solutions.

1. Argentic nitrate is dissolved in distilled water, and ammonia added to the solution till the precipitate first thrown down is almost entirely re-dissolved. The solution is filtered and diluted, so that 100 cc. contain one gramme of argentic nitrate.

N.B.—100 cc. are equal to rather more than $3\frac{1}{2}$ fluid ounces.

2. Two grammes of argentic nitrate are dissolved in a little distilled water, and poured into a litre of boiling distilled water. 1·66 gramme of Rochelle salt is added, and the mixture boiled for a short time, till the precipitate contained in it becomes grey; it is then filtered hot.

The glass, having been thoroughly cleaned with (1) nitric acid, (2) water, (3) caustic potash, (4) water, (5) alcohol, and lastly distilled water, is to be placed in a clean glass or porcelain vessel, the side to be silvered being placed uppermost. Equal quantities of the two solutions are then to be mixed and poured in, so as to cover the glass. This should be done while the glass is still wet with distilled water.

In about an hour the silvering will be completed. Then pour off the exhausted liquid, carefully remove glass, wash in clean water, rub off silver where deposited where not required, allow to dry, and varnish silvered side with any thin varnish which does not contract much in drying.

The time required for the operation depends on temperature.

If the solutions be warmed to about 30° C., the silver is deposited in a few minutes; but it is safer to use them cold.

The inside of test tubes, bulbs, &c., are silvered by putting the solutions into them, no second vessel being then required.

Throughout the whole operation the most scrupulous cleanliness is the grand essential.

100 cc. are equal to rather more than $3\frac{1}{2}$ fluid ounces.

1 gramme = 15·432 grains.

1 litre = $35\frac{1}{4}$ fluid ounces.

The plate of glass being thus carefully silvered is allowed to dry thoroughly, and is finally varnished with a good thick varnish, containing plenty of red lead, so that the back surface of the silver mirror has a smooth and red appearance, while the varnish protects the delicate film of metallic silver.

An ordinary photographic picture on glass is really represented by precipitated metallic silver, but the metal in this case is in minute particles, which do not shine or reflect light.

The silvered plate glass is now engraved in the following simple manner. Being placed in a support or rack against the wall, and quite upright, a chisel—or rather, a series of chisels—are drawn across the surface in straight lines, and perpendicular, by the use of a large T-square. Every time the chisel is drawn with pressure across the varnished back of the glass a portion of the silver is removed, leaving a straight line quite clear or transparent, and, in fact, laying bare the surface of the plate glass.

The lines were ruled in three degrees of comparison: thick, thicker, thickest; and considerable skill and experience —which no description can teach—were required to get these correctly engraved.

The engraved silver glass plate moved through a groove in the woodwork at the top of the chamber, and was supported below on a beautiful carriage, the wheels of which were covered with vulcanised indiarubber rings, and moved

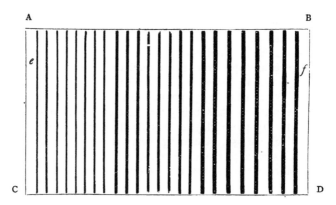

A B C D, the Plate Glass ; *e* straight lines engraved on silvered side and gradually increasing in thickness from *e* to *f.*

on a tramway below the floor of the room, perpendicularly. The glass could be made to slide at an angle of forty-five degrees, and as it always made a rumbling noise while moving, the music of the band concealed that defect. The ground plan of the apartment is shown on the opposite page.

Some idea of the cost of making a full-sized apparatus, with hangings and curtains and engraved glass, may be gathered from the fact that the author's outfit for Australia with a certain number of dresses cost £327 12s. 1d. Whilst the author was travelling through Australia Mr. James Walker, with his great inventive genius, made a further improvement, by which the concealed figure at K was done away with, and the whole apartment thrown open

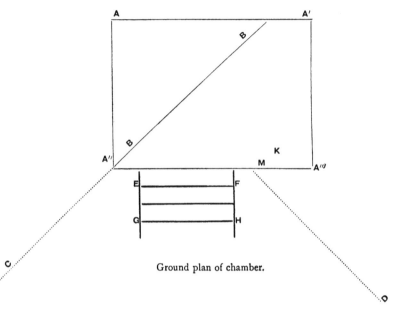

Ground plan of chamber.

A A′ A″ A‴, floor of the apartment ; B B, groove at an angle of 45°, in which the glass moved ; A″ to C groove continued outside of the apartment used when the glass was moved away ; E F G H, short flight of three or. four steps, as the room must stand some distance from the floor to allow of carriage moving on tramway.

N.B.—The groove A to C was concealed from the audience by handsome curtains, which were repeated at the same angle on the other side, from M to D.

K.—Place where the objects to be reflected in the looking-glass were placed, but quite concealed from the audience with a door, closed when the exhibition was going on.

to the public gaze. This was done to illustrate a clever
sketch written by Mr. Burnand called " Curried Prawns."

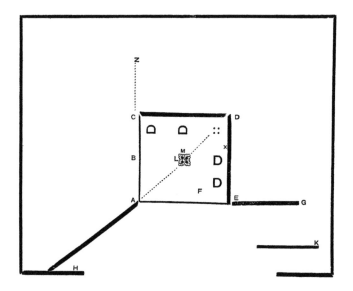

A C D E are the outside of the room, 12 feet square,
engraved glass running from H A to A D. The wing E G
is placed square ; this is an immense advantage, as it
renders unnecessary any counterpart at C N, and as, of
course, it cannot be seen, the light from the foot-lights on
E G is not seen by reflection at C N. When the wing E G
was at the same angle as H A, this was always a weak point
in the illusion, as when the glass crossed, the reflection
of E G, unless very dimly illuminated, always shewed. Now
it does not matter when E G is placed as in drawing.
The frontage to the audience, instead of being from A to F, is
now extended to E—*i.e.* 12 feet—consequently the return

sides F E and C B can be removed. This plan, of course, precludes the use of "trick" chairs, baskets, &c. &c. ; but it has a good many other advantages in its favour, for with a "sociable" in the middle of the room made in two exact halves, these halves trick or cover one another when the glass is pushed across, and of course this movement is not seen by the audience ; then any person or persons can be made to appear gradually, sitting or standing, at L or M, *right in the middle of the wide open room.* Mr. Walker tried this effect at the Polytechnic Institution, and it was capital—the ensemble is more imposing. This plan of shewing the illusion is the plan for the stage, as the necessity for darkening the stage in front is nearly wholly avoided. The back of the side-wing I K can be painted black, so that its reflection shall not be seen. In lieu of the gas-jets, as now arranged, there is a gas-lamp ; this is placed on a pedestal or small table. The shadow of the "sociable" to a great extent covers or hides the path along which the glass travels. Mr. Walker says : "I thought out this way for Mr. Irving's necessities, but I did not hear anything from him ; and it has come in well for Mr. Burnand's sketch, which has been produced." In this sketch, a gentleman afflicted with dyspepsia through eating "curried prawns " (the name of the piece), calling on some friends, where he has promised to help them in some amateur theatricals, looks at the different costumes of Mephistopheles, Faust and Marguerite, and throws them carelessly on the seat at M, walks down the steps (which we shall double in width) the glass now crosses, and, whilst in a fit of melancholy, he wonders if Mephistopheles will appear. Sure enough, he does. Mephistopheles then comes down in front, and with incantations makes, successively or together, Faust and Marguerite appear ; they then disappear in the same manner.

The author's friends and the public all know how

steadily he has opposed the so-called *Spiritual deceptions*, which generally are not a half nor a quarter as clever as the tricks of a first-rate conjuror.

Punch instructs us what to do at a Spiritual séance, which, if done, would certainly astonish the person performing the part of the materialised spirit. *Punch* writes— "How to behave at a Spiritual séance.—Always try to hit the happy Medium."

The author thought the time had now arrived when a new generation who knew not the ghost might be interested in its revival, and with that idea the authorities at the present Polytechnic concurred, so that by the time these pages are read it is hoped the ghost will be in full career once more, and if the author only receives a tenth part of the great patronage he received in 1863 he will be amply repaid for all his exertions in reproducing the ghost illusion. And he desires thankfully to acknowledge the very kind help he has received from Robert Mitchell, Esq., the Secretary and Manager of the numerous classes and useful lectures now so well conducted at Mr. Quintin Hogg's Polytechnic.

The author hopes to show "something new" at the Polytechnic; and a lady in miniature, as it were from Liliput, dances on a silver waiter held out by the author ; and the great man Napoleon I., for whom, like Alexander the Great, the world was too small, stands in the palm of the hand of the author.

If "duffers," &c., did not exist, the illusion would be explained to the public; but ten years need not elapse before they know all.

FINIS.

PRINTED BY CASSELL & COMPANY, LIMITED, LA BELLE SAUVAGE, LONDON, E.C.